CCSS **Genre** Realistic F

M000249655

Essential Question
What can learning about different cultures teach us?

by Hugh Brown
illustrated by Tim Jones

CHAPTER 1 Somewhere Special

"So, where are we going?" Carla asked as soon as she and her little brother, Mateo, were in the car.

"We're picking up Aunt Ceci at her house," their mother answered. "Then we're going somewhere special."

"Will it take us long to get there?" asked Mateo.

Their mother answered, "Not too long, but like I told you, it's a surprise." As she started the car, she added, "I *can* say that your Aunt Ceci has arranged a very special Tucson treat for us."

Aunt Ceci was Carla's favorite aunt—loud, confident, and with a great sense of style. Carla tried to imagine what the treat might be. She hoped it was an afternoon of shopping, because her aunt knew where to find the most interesting, quirky shops.

As they pulled up to Aunt Ceci's house, Carla saw her aunt waiting for them. "Maria, you are always late!" she laughed, embracing her sister as she got out of the car.

"I'm sorry," their mother apologized, "but the traffic was terrible."

"I know, it always is at this time of day," Ceci replied as she climbed into the passenger seat of the car. "We'll have to leave right away to get there in time."

Carla looked at her watch and wondered where they had to go. There must be some misunderstanding—the shops wouldn't close for hours yet.

As their mom pulled away from the curb, Ceci told them that one of Tucson's dance schools was hosting a festival. There would be performances by dancers from around the world. "It'll be a fabulous cultural event!" she said.

"Oh." Carla did her best to look pleased, but she felt disappointed because she had never been very interested in dancing. Even if the dancers were good, Carla couldn't imagine enjoying a whole festival that was just dancing.

Aunt Ceci saw the look on Carla's face and laughed. "Don't worry," she said. "I guarantee you'll enjoy it!"

When they arrived, Carla was surprised to see that a stage had been set up outside under tall, leafy trees. The sun shone through the branches, making a pattern of dappled light on the boards of the stage.

They found seats on the bleachers just as the first dancers came out wearing street clothes. Loud hip-hop music started playing, and Mateo grinned. But when the dancers started to move, they were not dancing hip-hop. They seemed to dance some kind of ballet, leaping and spinning gracefully across the stage.

Carla actually enjoyed watching them and listening to the music. As the performance continued, the dancers twirled and tumbled in dizzying combinations. Even Mateo was looking interested. Then suddenly the music ended, and the dance was over.

"What did you think of that?" Aunt Ceci asked eagerly as the dancers left the stage.

"It was interesting," Carla said casually, and Mateo just shrugged.

The next act started when three tall men dressed in black, one carrying a guitar, walked onto the stage. With a flourish of notes, the guitarist started playing. One of the other men raised his hands and began clapping out a rhythm.

Soon after, the third man started to sing. It was like nothing Carla had ever heard—a high, wailing song that sent shivers down her spine.

Mateo giggled, and Carla hissed, "Shush!" Embarrassed, she looked around, but everyone in the audience was focused on the stage. Carla turned back to the front where three women in long, colorful dresses strode out to take their places in front of the men.

The women started to move to the music. With their heads high and with fierce expressions on their faces, they strutted around the stage. Their feet pounded complicated rhythms with the heels of their shoes, and their hands twisted and turned in graceful motions.

"Wow," Mateo whispered, "they look so angry."

"They're not angry," Carla whispered back. "They're … proud and determined." Mateo was watching the dancers so intently that he did not hear what Carla said.

The dancers started to move faster, making their dresses whirl in a blur of color. Carla was fascinated by the dancers' controlled power and energy. She found herself sitting straighter in her chair, imitating their strong, erect posture.

When the performance was over, Aunt Ceci turned to Carla and Mateo and asked them what they thought.

"I thought all that stomping around was pretty weird," said Mateo.

"You did not!" contradicted Carla. "You were so busy watching that you didn't even hear me when I spoke to you." She turned to her aunt. "It was wonderful, Aunt Ceci! They were just so …"

Before she could think of the right word, a new group of dancers came on. They were good, but Carla could not stop thinking about the dance that she had just seen.

CHAPTER 2 It's Called Flamenco

On the way back to Aunt Ceci's house, Carla peppered her aunt with questions about the second dance group.

"They were dancing flamenco—that dance group comes from Mexico," Aunt Ceci explained.

"From Mexico, like our family," Carla said, pleased to have a personal connection to the wonderful dancers.

Aunt Ceci continued, "Flamenco was originally brought to Latin America by the Spanish, but now lots of other people dance flamenco and play the music, too."

"Aunt Ceci learned flamenco dancing from our grandma—your great-grandmother," added Carla's mother. "Ceci also took lessons from a traditional teacher when she was a girl in Mexico."

Carla's eyes lit up. "You know how to dance like that, Aunt Ceci?" she asked in amazement. "Do you think you could teach me?"

"You can't dance!" snorted Mateo.

"Don't be so critical, Mat," their mother scolded.

Aunt Ceci agreed to show Carla a couple of steps, but she warned, "I haven't danced for a long time, and I wasn't always a very good student, I'm afraid. As a girl, I didn't have much appreciation for our heritage."

When they arrived at Aunt Ceci's house, they pushed back the chairs and sofa in the living room to make more space. Mateo and his mother went to sit on the porch.

Aunt Ceci explained to Carla that to start, they would use just their feet. Then she told Carla, "Put your hands on your hips and stomp on the floor. Use your right foot twice, then the left, then the right twice again. Now repeat that the other way around—two left, right, two left, right."

Aunt Ceci stomped out the rhythm to show Carla, then she laughed. "It's supposed to make a loud noise," she said, "but I forgot about the carpet!"

Ceci thought for a moment, then added, "I remember now—Grandma called the stomping steps *golpes*."

Carla copied both patterns with her feet.

"Fantastic! You're picking it up so quickly," Aunt Ceci praised. "Okay, now we'll add in the arms." She made big, bold movements with her arms while keeping the rhythm going with her feet.

After they had been practicing for a while, Aunt Ceci told Carla, "I think you have a real talent for dance, and you should consider taking lessons. It would be wonderful to have a flamenco dancer in the family again."

She was still complimenting Carla's dancing ability as they headed outside to the porch. "You should congratulate this one, Maria," Aunt Ceci said. "She did very well."

"It's fun," Carla said. "Thanks for the lesson, Aunt Ceci, and for taking us to the festival, too. You were right—it was fabulous."

All the way home in the car, Carla's feet were tapping out the rhythms her aunt had taught her. She also thought about the dancers she had seen, trying to remember as many of their movements as she could. She imagined herself dancing on the stage.

When they got home, it was just about bedtime. Before getting into bed, Carla quickly practiced again, using her arms and feet together as her aunt had shown her.

The next day after school, Carla asked her mother, "May I use the computer? There's some research I want to do."

"Sure," her mother answered. "Speaking of research, there's something that I need to find out. Is there anything you would particularly like for your birthday next week?" Her mother smiled.

"Flamenco!" Carla blurted out. "I mean, flamenco lessons. Please." Carla held her breath as she waited to see what her mother would say.

Her mother looked surprised and pleased. But all she said was, "We'll see. We have to find out how much it costs and when the lessons are."

"That's the research that I was just going to do on the Internet!" Carla said.

"We can do it together then," her mother said.

So Carla searched for dance schools in their area that taught flamenco, and her mother jotted down the phone numbers. She promised Carla that she would call them and get more information.

CHAPTER 3 A Birthday Surprise

Carla asked her mother the next day if she had called about dance lessons. Her mother replied, "I'm still thinking about it. Please don't nag me, Carla."

Every day, Carla practiced the steps that her aunt had shown her. Once, her mother came into her room while she was practicing. Even then her mother didn't say anything about lessons. Carla was beginning to think her mother had totally forgotten about her interest in flamenco classes.

The day before Carla's birthday, her mother picked her up after school as usual. But instead of going home, they headed downtown.

"Where are we going?" Carla asked.

"I think you can guess what I'm going to say to that," her mother replied, chuckling.

"Wait and see?" Carla suggested. Her mother nodded.

Carla didn't have to wait long to find out. A few minutes later, they parked the car, and she followed her mother to a large two-story building.

"What's this place?" Carla asked. Then she noticed the poster in the window near the entrance. It said, "Learn to dance Flamenco!"

Her mother hadn't forgotten! Carla hugged her. "Thanks, Mom!" she beamed.

Her mother went to the trunk of the car and took out a duffel bag and a wrapped present. "Happy birthday, Carla. I'm very proud of how much you've been practicing what Aunt Ceci showed you." She handed Carla the box and told her to open it when they got inside.

"Inside?" Carla asked. "Am I having a lesson right now?" Her mother nodded, and Carla was suddenly nervous. "But I don't have anything to wear—just my school clothes."

"Don't worry," her mother told her. "I brought some clothes for you." They went inside and climbed the stairs to the dance studio on the second floor.

Carla couldn't help feeling worried. She imagined that the teacher would be stern and fierce-looking like the women at the dance festival. When they reached the studio at the top of the stairs, Carla's mother paused and asked Carla, "Are you ready?"

Carla was so nervous that she almost asked her mother if they could come back another day. Then she remembered how she had felt watching the dancers. She thought about how excited she had been to learn that they were from Mexico, like her family. She also thought about how proud it made her feel that her great-grandmother had been a flamenco dancer, and her aunt, too.

She turned to her mother and did her best to smile bravely. "I'm ready," she said.

When they went inside, the teacher came over to them right away. She did not look fierce at all but smiled warmly at Carla. "You must be Carla and Maria," she said. "The changing rooms are over here."

Carla still felt nervous and asked her mother if she was going to stay and watch. Then Carla looked down at the shoes her mother was taking out of her bag. "Mom, those aren't my shoes, they're yours!" she said, confused.

Her mother smiled. "Watching those dancers at the festival reminded me how much I wanted to learn flamenco when I was a girl. Unfortunately, Grandma was too old to teach me by the time I was big enough to learn."

She handed some clothes to Carla. "You don't mind if I take the class with you, do you?"

All Carla's nervousness disappeared. "No! I'd love for you to learn, too. I didn't really want you to leave," she admitted.

Carla changed her clothes while her mother put on some hard-soled shoes with a heel that she thought would make a good noise. When she was dressed Carla looked in the bag again. "You forgot my shoes," she said. "Will my sneakers be all right?"

Her mother reminded her that she hadn't opened her present yet.

"Maybe I should wait until after the class," Carla said. "We don't want to be late."

"I think there's time," her mother said.

Carla ripped off the paper and opened the box. Inside was a pair of bright red, hard-soled shoes with tiny nails hammered into the heels.

"Oh—flamenco shoes!" Carla breathed. "They're beautiful!"

"Put them on," her mother said. "And then let's go make your great-grandmother proud."

Respond to Reading

Summarize

Use the most important details from *Dancing the Flamenco* to summarize the story. Your graphic organizer may help.

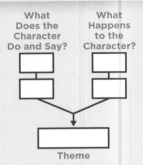

Text Evidence

1. What features of *Dancing the Flamenco* help you identify it as realistic fiction? **GENRE**

2. What do Carla and her mother learn about themselves from the flamenco show? Based on this, what do you think the author's main message is? **THEME**

3. What is the meaning of the word *dappled* on page 4? Use the cause-and-effect relationship in the paragraph to help you figure out the meaning. **CONTEXT CLUES: CAUSE AND EFFECT**

4. Write about the message the author is trying to tell readers by showing Carla's reaction to the flamenco performance in Chapter 2. **WRITE ABOUT READING**

Compare Texts

Read about the history of flamenco.

Flamenco-style dance is from a region in Spain called Andalusia. It is thought that Gypsies from India, who moved to Andalusia, brought their style of singing and dancing with them. These became mixed with the music and dance of Andalusia, and the result was flamenco. Eventually, people in many parts of Spain started to sing and dance flamenco.

Where Flamenco Began

SPAIN

Andalusia

INDIA

The word *flamenco* does not just refer to dancing. The three main things that make up a flamenco performance are singing (called *cante* in Spanish), dancing (or *baile*), and instrumental music, which is usually played on the guitar. There is often hand-clapping to add percussion to the music, too.

The singing might sound unusual to people who have not heard it before because songs are sung in a mix of Spanish and a Gypsy dialect called *Caló*. The unusual sound of flamenco singing also is the result of using scales, or patterns of notes, that are different from other Western music. Flamenco singers have a "wailing" style of singing, which is used to express strong emotions.

Both men and women dance flamenco, but the way they dance is slightly different. The men traditionally focus on footwork, tapping and stomping out complex rhythms. The women's part is a mixture of footwork and movements made with their upper bodies, arms, and hands.

Sometimes the dance tells the story of the song that is being sung.

Flamenco dancers convey a sense of pride when they dance.

Flamenco guitar was originally played to accompany the singer and dancers. It is so popular these days that it has now become a solo instrumental style. Some flamenco guitarists give concerts where there is no singing or dancing at all.

Flamenco Around the World

Carla is not the only person to become caught up in the magic of flamenco. People all around the world love the melodies, rhythms, power, and beauty of this style of music and dance.

You can find people dancing flamenco wherever you go—including places without a history of Spanish influence. There is even a flamenco dance craze in Japan!

This woman from Japan is dancing Flamenco.

Make Connections

What cultures have contributed to the development of flamenco? ESSENTIAL QUESTION

Compare how the flamenco singing style is described in *Dancing the Flamenco* and in *Flamenco*.
TEXT TO TEXT

Focus on Literary Elements

Dialogue Authors use dialogue to show readers what characters say. Dialogue can help move the plot along and indicate action. Comic strips are an example of the way a story can be told just by using dialogue and illustrations.

Read and Find In this piece of dialogue from page 6, the author tells us what the characters say and what they are doing. As you read it, think about the images that could help tell the story.

When the performance was over, Aunt Ceci turned to Carla and Mateo and asked them what they thought.

"I thought all that stomping around was pretty weird," said Mateo.

"You did not!" contradicted Carla. "You were so busy watching that you didn't even hear me when I spoke to you." She turned to her aunt. "It was wonderful, Aunt Ceci! They were just so ..."

Your Turn

Now turn this, or another section of dialogue, into a comic strip. Use the words the characters say and add at least six drawings of your own. Then share your comic strip with your classmates.